printmaking

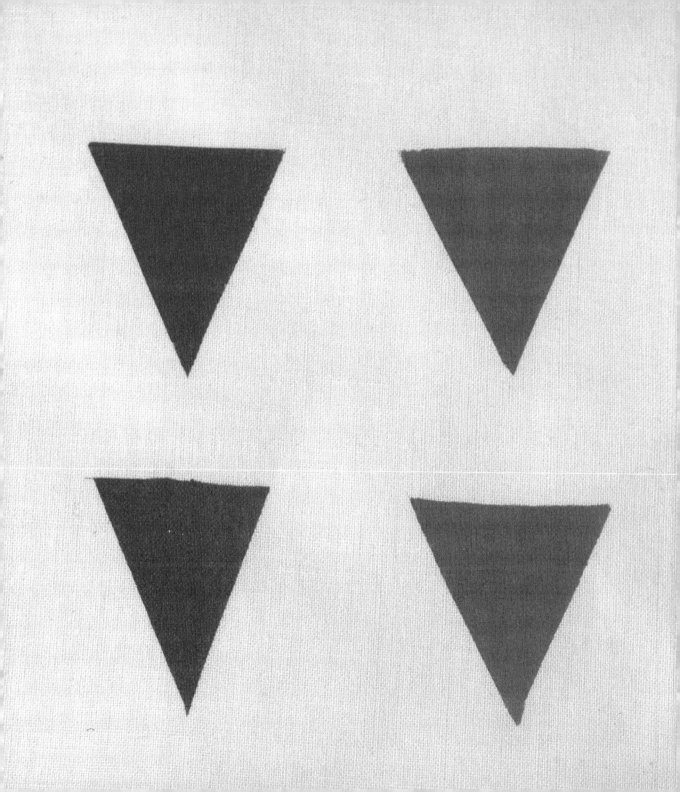

printmaking

20 projects for friends to make

super+super

First published 2014 by
Guild of Master Craftsman Publications Ltd
Castle Place, 166 High Street, Lewes,
East Sussex BN7 1XU

ISBN 978 1 86108 979 3

A catalogue record for this book is available from the
British Library.

Publisher: Jonathan Bailey
Production Manager: Jim Bulley
Managing Editor: Gerrie Purcell
Senior Project Editor: Wendy McAngus
Editor: Jane Roe
Managing Art Editor: Gilda Pacitti
Art Editor: Rebecca Mothersole
Illustrator: Anna-Kaisa Jormanainen
Photographers: Claire Culley, Rebecca Mothersole
and Harry Watts

Set in Akzidenz-Grotesk, Ani Lazy Day and Calibri
Colour origination by GMC Reprographics
Printed and bound in China

contents

Introduction to printing

Printing is a huge part of our everyday lives. From letters and newspapers to paper money, it's crucial for sharing information and key for most aspects of our lives. Professional printing is a mass-manufactured industry, but it's not these aspects that are capturing the attentions of many a crafter at the moment. Everyone wants to jump on the printing bandwagon, and quite rightly so, we say!

There is nothing more satisfying than learning a new skill and then using that skill to make something amazing. Whether it be for a gift, for a project or just for you to put around your home, it's fun (and messy) for all.

There are so many different printing processes out there for you to learn. From simple stamp printing to more labour-intensive lino printing, there really is something for every crafter, at every level, and you'll soon find that you have your own favourite technique.

Art prints, fabrics, homewares and stationery are all examples of printed objects that, with a little bit of guidance, are easy to reproduce at home. You may not be able to re-create them on a huge scale but we'll show you a few tricks of the trade that will have you printing away in no time.

The brilliant thing about printing is that there's no hard or fast rule about how something should look. You can 'freestyle' to your heart's content until you have an effect that you are happy with. You can mix your own colours, make your own repeat patterns, overlay designs and much more. Your creativity will be soaring through the roof!

Amy & Claire, Super+Super

Get your paint pots out

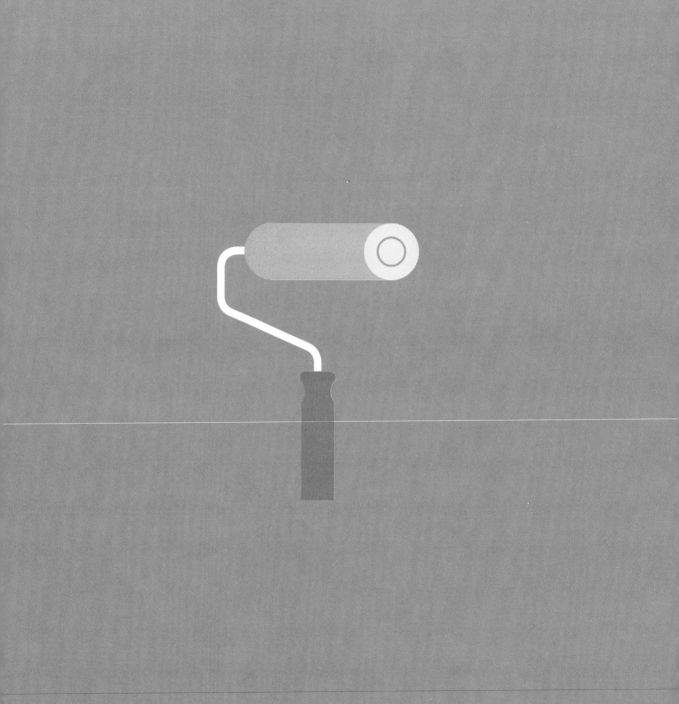

····*(!)*····

ready, steady, make

Using this book

This book is a collection of 20 projects of varying levels of difficulty. We want you to bring your own style to each project by thrifting, reusing and swapping materials and colours.

Our aim is to help novice crafters to become more confident designer-makers in a series of manageable projects. We encourage everyone to push each project to the next level by adding and extending where it appeals to them, adding their own stamp of personality. We hope that this book inspires you to get creative and share your brilliant new skills!

The book is divided into four sections – lazy crafter, weeknight winner, perpetual creative and committed crafter. The sections are based on timescales so you can make sure you have enough time to finish a project before you start it. There's nothing worse than a half-finished project or feeling like you have to rush something.

Lazy crafter

These give you a few simple makes for the minimum time and effort. These projects are great for getting you into the swing of something new or for a quick creative fix when you have a few precious moments to spare.

Weeknight winners

This chapter has a selection of projects that are short enough to be completed in a single evening and can be made with items that are readily found around a crafter's home. They are ideal for an evening in alone or with a group of friends at a crafty get-together.

Perpetual creative

These medium-length projects will keep you inspired over a quiet weekend (or two) for when you need a creative intermission to an often hectic working week.

Committed crafter

These longer-length, more complex projects can be enjoyed at your leisure over an extended period of time, maybe a holiday or sabbatical. They are perfect for improving your skills base.

Before you start printing make sure you have the right type of workspace. It can be a messy process, so be prepared with wipe-clean tablecloths or newspaper to protect your work surface. You will also find that for some of the projects you may need an extra pair of hands to hold screens steady or help you to apply even pressure. Why not organize a 'crafternoon' with friends so you can all help each other and hang out at the same time?

Sometimes printing can be a bit hit and miss so don't be too downhearted if something doesn't come out exactly how you imagined it. It really is trial and error some of the time and you may even find that a mistake turns into a happy accident!

We encourage creativity with all of these projects and there is always scope to add more to each design should you wish to. Perhaps you could add a touch of embroidery to the homeware projects, change the ink colours or even customize your banner with your own favourite phrase. The possibilities are endless. We are just here to inspire!

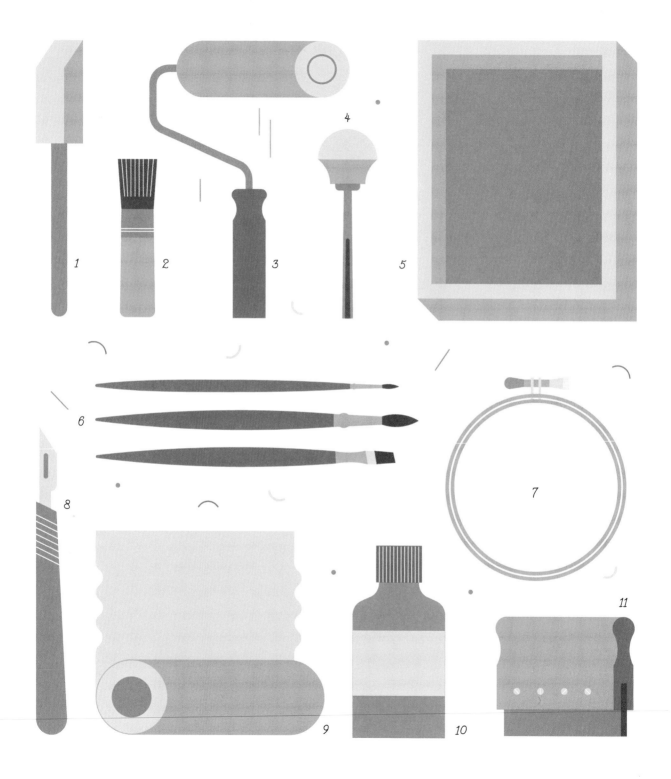

What you'll need

Chances are you will already have almost all of the basic equipment needed for these projects at home. However, if you are missing some items, why not beg or borrow any additional equipment for projects you are underprepared for? You must return things in the same state as they were in when they were acquired, of course! In all of our projects we have tried to stick to the bare essentials and have included thrifty options for the basics, which can be picked up cheaply from art stores, craft shops, charity shops (thift stores) and stationers. Even supermarkets stock basic stationery items nowadays too.

printing tools

1   Painting sponge
This is handy for dabbing paint and ink onto stencils and linocuts. You can use a normal paintbrush instead.

2   Stencilling brush
These are available in a wide range of different shapes and sizes and can be bought from most art and craft shops.

3   Roller
You don't need anything specialized or expensive – a simple sponge roller will help to get an even coverage of ink. You will also need a hard roller or brayer for lino printing.

4   Linocut tool
This is found in art shops and online craft stores. Look for one with a simple handle and interchangeable blades.

5   Screen-printing screen
Where we haven't given a DIY option, try eBay as a source for used screens. Before purchasing a used screen, make sure it doesn't already have a design on it.

6   Paintbrushes
A fine paintbrush is a useful tool to have on hand for projects requiring precision. It can be used to fill in any small details and is especially good for the drawing fluid technique (see page 26). Thicker ones are handy for filling in bigger areas.

7   Embroidery hoop
These hoops make perfect DIY screens for printing through. Try scouring charity shops (thrift stores) or boot fairs and garage sales for them. You'll be surprised how many you can pick up for a bargain.

8   Scalpel
If you're likely to use it a lot, we would recommend a handle with detachable blades. Scalpels are very sharp so be extra careful when changing the blades. If you want something less intimidating, you can buy simple craft knives from your local art store, but look for one that doesn't have detachable mini blades. These can be tricky to use as you will find the case slips down when you are using it, which is not productive at all.

9   43T mesh count silk
This silk is ideal for making your own screen with an embroidery hoop. You can find it in a haberdashery department or online.

10   Removable screen block
This clay-like substance is used in conjunction with drawing fluid for creating your screen design.

11   Squeegee
For some projects it's best to use a medium-sized squeegee so you can cover the design in one swoop. Little plastic squeegees are usually used for applying vinyl to windows, but are also great for small prints. They are super cheap too.

basic equipment

1 Fabric scissors

You will need a pair of good-quality, super-sharp fabric scissors for cutting fabrics. Make sure you use these scissors on fabrics only as they blunt easily if used on paper or card.

2 General scissors

You will need a general-purpose pair of scissors for cutting paper, card and ends.

3 Pinking shears

Pinking shears are specialized scissors that cut with a zigzag edge. These stop edges from fraying and are a huge timesaver when you don't have time to hem edges.

4 Pencil and pen

You don't need an expensive pencil, just an ordinary one will be fine. It's also handy to have a pen, felt tip or permanent marker to hand.

5 Spoon

An old teaspoon or a dessert spoon is the perfect tool for applying your ink before printing.

6 Ruler

A regular ruler will suffice, but a steel ruler is more helpful due to its weight and durability. You will also need a cutting mat to use with it when you are cutting straight lines with your scalpel. An A4 size will work for all the projects in this book but you may find it easier to work on a larger one.

7 Tracing paper

Tracing paper is used for tracing templates to make stencils.

8 Brown paper

This can be used to make your stencils with. It's most economical to buy brown paper as a roll and one roll should keep you going for a long time.

9 Plain paper

Having some plain A4 paper on hand will be helpful, whether it's for doodling design ideas, practising your printing and stamping techniques or simply for covering your work surface.

10 Medium to thick card

Medium to thick card is mainly used for creating your own stencil shapes for the stencilling printing technique. The card will be more durable for repeat printing.

11 Tape measure

Either a steel or fabric tape measure will be handy for measuring distances or checking that stencils are centred.

12 Adhesive and masking tapes

Sticky tape is a must for your printing bag as it is frequently used for securing stencils and templates in place. Always try to buy good-quality masking tape as there's nothing more disappointing than masking tape that doesn't stick properly or lift off cleanly.

13 Eraser

Useful for correcting any little errors you make along the way.

14 Kitchen knife

You will need a sharp knife for making stamps out of food items.

Tip! Printmaking is a messy business so make sure you have plenty of newspaper and plastic bags to hand. They will come in handy for protecting your work area and making sure you print only on the surfaces you mean to print on!

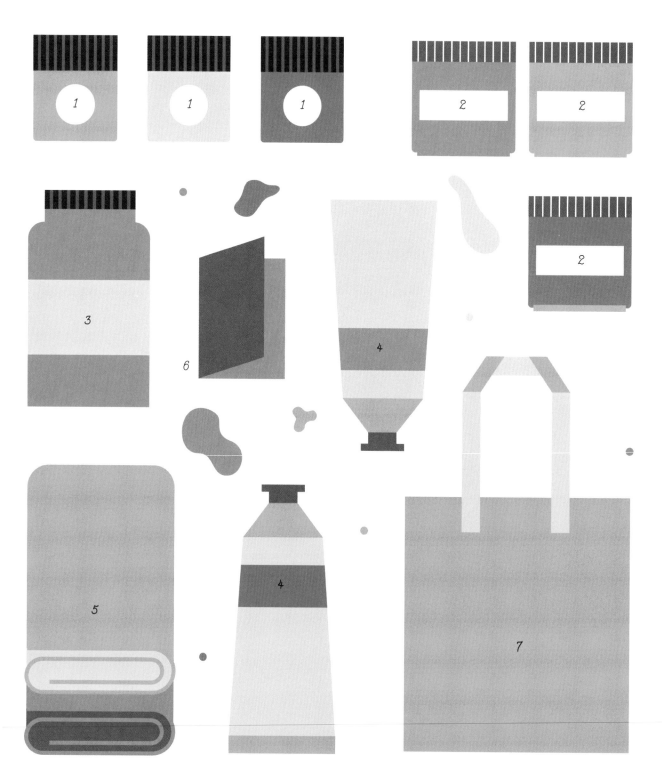

paints and inks

1 Screen-printing fabric inks

It's important to use specialized screen-printing ink when making a screen print. The advanced polymer technology combined with pure pigments creates a professional finish like no other. When using these inks, it's important to seal the ink afterwards with heat. Do this by placing paper or a piece of light fabric over the print and ironing over it.

2 Fabric paint

Little pots of fabric paint are great for the stamp-printing technique (see page 20). They come in such an amazing range of colours that it's difficult not to get addicted to using them! As with screen-printing inks, you need to seal the fabric afterwards with cloth and an iron.

3 Drawing fluid

This is used to create prints on silk screens. Drawing fluid acts as a barrier to the screen filler. It can be used with stencils or freehand drawing.

4 Acrylics

We use acrylics for a lot of our card-based projects. The great thing about acrylics is that they are water based so they can be mixed with water to thin them down and it's easier to clean your brushes or screens. They are made from pigments mixed with acrylic resin and emulsion and are therefore very fast drying.

Tip! Old cups, bowls and other containers will come in handy for mixing your printing inks. It's best to pick something you don't plan to eat or drink from again.

media

5 Fabrics

Generally the projects in this book are upcycling projects so you won't have to source specific fabric. But you will need to give some thought to how suitable the fabric is that you will be printing onto. If the fabric is too dark, for example, a dark-coloured ink will not show up well. Cottons are generally the best and most effective fabrics to print onto.

Calico is widely available and is a great material to print onto. It's a good idea to iron it before printing to get all the creases out. Calico is extremely versatile and is especially suited for prints, which you can then frame and hang on the wall.

6 Cards

There is no need to buy expensive cards and envelopes for any of our projects unless you wish to. Large packs of cards are available at discount outlets and stationers aplenty.

7 Cotton tote bag

A couple of the projects in this book use tote bags. Where possible we urge you to recycle an old tote you no longer use, especially if the back of the bag has no design. If you don't have a spare tote bag, why not check out the local charity or thrift shop or ask a friend.

How to do it

There are so many printing techniques to try. In this section, we'll give you a brief overview of each of the methods used in the book so you can be fully prepared before diving into the projects.

stamp printing

Stamp or relief printing is the perfect introduction to printing. You can buy lots of different types of stamps from craft shops or you can make your own stamp using different household items. Throughout this book we make our own stamps from potatoes, apples, string and even just a simple pencil eraser. This is a fun technique for crafters of all ages.

The easiest way to stamp print is to use an ink block of your colour choice, press the stamp gently into the ink and then straight onto your piece of card or paper. Stamp away to your heart's content until you are happy with your design.

When stamping onto fabric, it is important to use fabric paint (see page 19), which is widely available from art shops, craft shops and online. Once you have printed your design onto the fabric, you will need to seal the ink with a hot iron on the reverse of the fabric. Doing this means you can wash and reuse your fabric over and over again.

When making your own stamp, particularly if you are making it out of a food item, it's important to take care as you will need a sharp knife to cut your desired shape out. Use a cutting board and take your time. Stamps made from food won't last for too long due to their moisture content, so if you are working on a big design, you may need a large supply of potatoes or apples to keep it looking sharp.

STAMP PRINT FROM
APPLE TEA TOWEL, PAGE 56

LINO PRINT FROM MULTI-PRINT
WALLPAPER, PAGE 102

lino printing

Linocut printing is probably the most time-consuming of all the printing techniques but once you get the hang of it, it's really fun and very rewarding. What's more, your linocut can then be used over and over again.

Linocuts are very similar to woodcuts in that you use tools to scrape away parts of the lino, leaving the parts of the design you wish to be inked. To create your own lino print, you will firstly need the right tools and equipment.

Linoleum sheet can be bought from most art shops. It's best to use the grey coloured one as this is the most effective; the pink or white coloured sheets are made from rubber and are not suitable for carving. Lino-cutting tools include a sponge, which is used to evenly transfer your ink onto the lino cut. A hard roller, sometimes called a brayer, is used to press the surface you are printing on evenly over the linocut. The surface you are printing on determines the type of paint you will need. Acrylic paint is best for printing onto more hardwearing, thicker surfaces or plastics. Gouache or watercolour paints can be used for fine-art prints and water-based paints are ideal for thinner papers. Fabric paint should be used for woven, felted or knitted fabrics.

To make your linocut, start by drawing your design onto the lino with a pencil. Remember to reverse the design – that is, a mirror image – especially if you are printing letters, because they will print the other way round. Next, use a craft knife to go round the design, this makes it a lot easier for when you start cutting away with the lino tool at the space you don't want to print.

Using the V-blade in your lino tool, you can now start to go around the edge of the design. Take care to dig out small pieces of the lino until you get into the swing of it. Always push away from you with the blade to avoid any nasty nicks on your fingers.

Once the edge of the design has been revealed, you can start to use the U-blade for the rest of the design. Be careful not to push too deep and reveal the backing. Once it is finished the area you want to print, called the positive part of the design, will be raised up ready to be inked and the rest of the lino (the negative space) will have been cut back deeper.

Use a sponge to evenly distribute the ink onto the design. Then turn the lino over and place it onto your chosen material. Use a hard roller to roll over the backing. This will create an even print. Remove your lino to reveal your print.

Repeat this process as often as needed to complete your pattern.

screen printing

This technique uses a woven mesh to transfer your design. Screen printing creates a professional outcome that is widely used for clothing, homewares and art prints. Screen printing is fun (and a little bit messy at times) but once you have got the hang of it, it's easy to do and very addictive!

In this book we use the stencil style of screen printing. However, if you get the bug, there are other types of printing you can learn.

To create your stencil you will need a scalpel or craft knife, a cutting mat and a piece of brown paper. Cut your stencil out of the paper, making sure to cut onto the mat to protect the work surface. You will also find the cutting mat makes it easier to cut curves and smoother lines.

Stencils made in this way are temporary so you will only be able to produce a few prints from them. Once your stencil has been made, you can choose what you would like to print onto. If you are printing onto paper or card, use acrylic or screen-printing ink. Use fabric ink if you are printing onto fabric. Remember you will need to seal any prints onto fabric with a hot iron on the reverse side.

Start by laying your chosen material onto a wipe-clean tablecloth or a piece of newspaper to protect your work surface. Now place your stencil over the material, taking time to make sure it is in the right place, and is straight, not crumpled. Carefully lay the screen over the top of your stencil. Use a spoon to spread the ink over the top of the design – about an inch (2.5cm) from the top should do the trick. Now grab your squeegee ready for pulling. The easiest way to hold the squeegee is with both hands and at a 45° angle to the design. Using a firm and fluid motion and with some pressure, pull the squeegee over the ink to the bottom of your design. The squeegee will push the ink through the mesh, revealing a positive print where the stencil has been cut out.

Sometimes it is necessary to repeat this process if you can see the ink hasn't taken over the whole design. Now reveal your print and leave to dry.

SCREEN PRINTING FROM CUCKOO
CLOCK ART PRINT, PAGE 70

*DRAWING-FLUID TECHNIQUE FROM
MONOGRAMMED TABLET CASE, PAGE 98*

drawing-fluid technique

This technique is perfect for creating a line drawing or a more detailed design.

You can make your own screen using 43T mesh count silk, or buy a ready-made silk screen. Start by attaching your stencil to the underside of the screen with adhesive tape. You can skip this step if you prefer to paint by eye.

Ensure that the design is back to front at this point so it will be the right way round when you turn the screen back over.

Use a small paintbrush and drawing fluid to paint the design, then leave it to dry overnight.

The next day you need to cover the screen in the removable screen block. Use your squeegee to create an even coverage. Once again, you will need to leave this to dry overnight.

When you come back to it a day later, wash the screen block off using warm water to reveal your design. Take care when doing this and don't rub too hard.

The design should reveal itself with a little gentle persuasion with a sponge. Once the screen dries, you will have an exposed design to print with.

To print your design, place your chosen material down on a table, place the screen on top and spoon some ink along the top of the design. Ask a friend or family member to hold the screen down as you pull the squeegee over the design in a firm and fluid motion. Remove the screen to reveal your print.

STENCIL PRINT FROM CHEVRON
PLACE MATS, PAGE 74

stencil printing

Stencil printing is extremely versatile and if you have the right brush and the right inks you can stencil onto almost anything. In this book we have shown how to stencil with card and even just masking tape. It's suitable for all levels of ability. Have fun creating different types of stencils whether this is text, shapes or block designs.

For stencil printing you will need a proper stencil brush. These come in a range of different shapes and sizes and can be bought from most art and craft shops and even some stationers. The main technique to master for stencilling is holding your brush correctly. It's important to hold your brush vertically at a 90° angle to the stencil. Think of it as dabbing rather than painting. Always start with less ink or paint on your brush

than you think is necessary as it's better to build up the colour gradually rather than having too much at first.

You can stencil onto all types of media; just make sure you have the correct paint to do so. When painting onto card or paper, use poster paints or acrylic paint and for fabrics use fabric inks only.

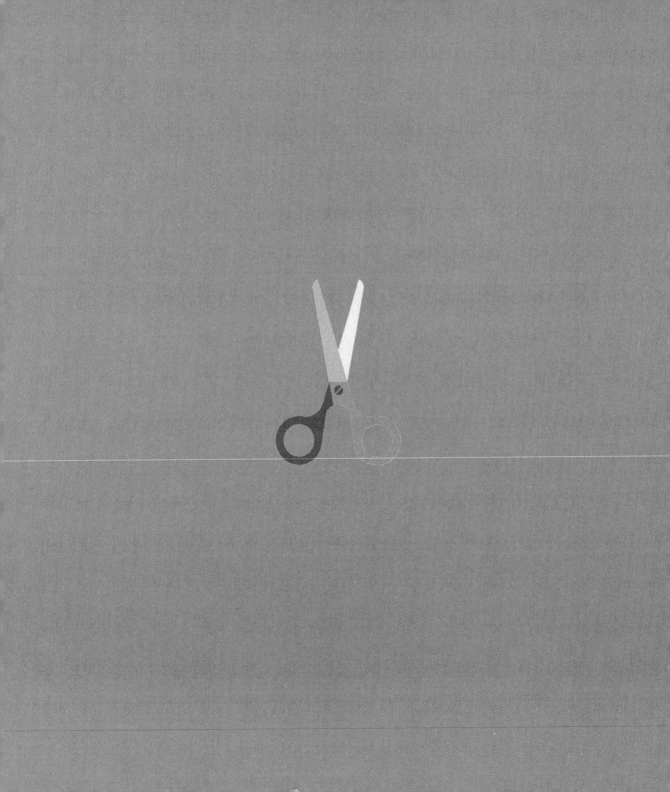

¿\¡/·/ ! \·\¡/ ;

lazy crafter

¿/!\·\ ¡ /·/!\¿

Bleach-dotted jeans

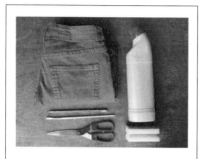

WHAT YOU NEED

- ☐ Pair of old denim jeans
- ☐ Thick bleach
- ☐ Sponge
- ☐ Paintbrush
- ☐ Scissors
- ☐ Pencil

Update that tired old pair of jeans with a simple abstract dot project. Transform your look instantly with this season's must-have.

1 Cover your work surface with newspaper and tuck some folded plastic bags into the legs of your jeans. This will stop the bleach soaking through onto the other side of the garment. Cut your sponge into finger-sized chunks and fill an old cup or bowl with a few inches of bleach, stirring it gently with the paintbrush. Bleach is very caustic so do be careful – it's a good idea to wear rubber gloves.

2 Dip the end of your sponge into the bleach, wiping any excess off on the side of the cup. Dab with a light, even pressure onto the fabric for a second next to the zip and then lift the sponge off. Sponge a row of four even spots along the top of the jeans underneath the pocket.

3 Now stagger the following row of dots so that they are in the middle of the space between the two above. You can plan out the position with the pencil. Continue staggering the dots in this way all down the length of the first leg and then repeat on the second.

4 Leave to dry, then machine wash at a cold setting to remove any active bleach. Be aware that the colour will continue to get lighter as the bleach develops.

Tip! Reload the sponge with bleach before each new application to maintain even dots.

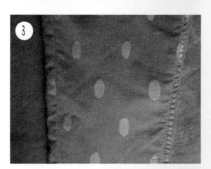

Tip! Wash your jeans as soon as the bleach is dry. If the bleach is left on for too long, holes could form where it burns all the way through the fabric.

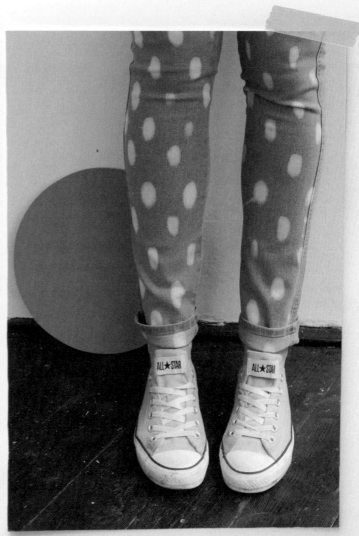

Toothbrush smudge napkins

WHAT YOU NEED

- ☐ Heavy cotton or linen napkins
- ☐ Old toothbrush
- ☐ Screen-print or fabric-painting ink

Tip! Once dry, press a hot iron onto the reverse of your design to heat seal the ink and make the napkins washproof

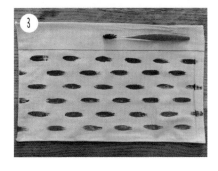

Lend a chic look to any dinner party with these napkins inspired by traditional Ikat designs. Using a toothbrush to smudge on the design gives a pared-down yet authentic woven effect.

1 Dip the bristles of your old toothbrush into a pot of your chosen ink.

2 Now firmly press the loaded brush onto the fabric of your napkin and drag it a little in one direction, left or right, and then lift off.

3 Repeat this step as many times as you desire, placing each mark approximately 2in (5cm) apart in a line along the width of your fabric. Repeat this process in staggered lines down the length of the napkin, creating a striking repeat pattern. Decorate other napkins in the same way, using different colours if the mood takes you.

TOOTHBRUSH SMUDGE
NAPKINS, PAGE 32

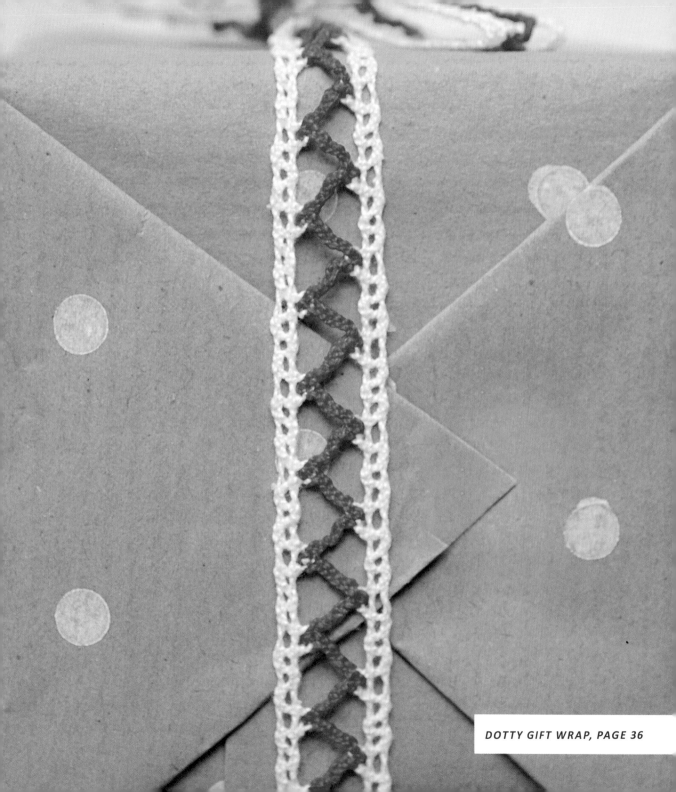

DOTTY GIFT WRAP, PAGE 36

Dotty gift wrap

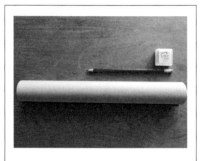

WHAT YOU NEED

- ☐ Brown paper
- ☐ Pencil with an unused eraser on the end
- ☐ Ink pad of your chosen colour

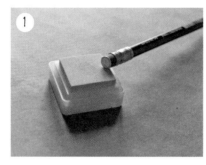

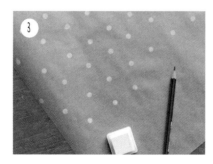

This simple project is a really sweet way to transform any gift. You can make this with any item found around the house. And for the finishing touch, why not add contrasting or complementary ribbons for a little extra something?

1 Start by cutting the brown paper to the desired size. Then spread the paper out onto a table, using a few heavy objects to hold down the corners. Take your pencil and lightly push the eraser end into the ink pad.

2 Now use the rubber as a stamp to create your first dots.

3 Repeat this process until the paper is covered.

Tip! Try stamping with different coloured ink pads to add a multicoloured polka dot effect to your gift wrap.

('weeknight winners')

Raindrop baby sleepsuit

WHAT YOU NEED

- [ ] Cotton sleepsuit
- [ ] Potato
- [ ] Scalpel or kitchen knife
- [ ] Non-toxic fabric paint or screen-printing ink
- [ ] Sponge roller
- [ ] Non-toxic felt-tip pen
- [ ] Paintbrush

Give a little one's wardrobe a playful update with this simple as you like print project. Perfect for brightening up tired whites, it also makes a fantastic gift so why not make two, or even more?

1   Line your sleepsuit with plastic bags so that the ink does not leak through onto the inside. Cut the potato in half and discard one piece. Using the felt tip pen, draw a raindrop shape onto the flat side of the potato.

2   Cut around this shape with the knife, tracing the outline. Then cut away all the potato surrounding the shape to a depth of approximately $3/16$ in (5mm).

3   Pour some of your chosen fabric paint or screen-printing ink into an old saucer. Load your sponge roller with the paint or ink and paint onto the potato stamper.

4   Print onto the sleepsuit using a firm and even pressure and making sure you reload the stamp with ink before each press.

5   Print randomly all over the front of the sleepsuit until you have got the look you want.

Tip! Leave to dry for 24 hours and then iron on high on the reverse side to seal the ink.

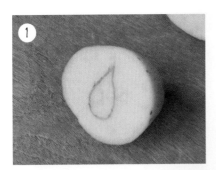

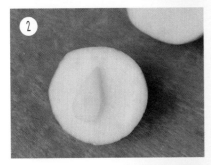

Geometric cushion

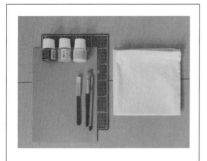

WHAT YOU NEED

- [ ] Plain cushion cover
- [ ] Fabric inks
- [ ] Card
- [ ] Cutting mat
- [ ] Scalpel or craft knife
- [ ] Pencil
- [ ] Stencil brush

This bright stencilling project is the perfect way to play around with block colours and layering. Create a bold print effect in no time at all in four easy steps.

1 Start by making your stencils. Draw your chosen shapes on the card using a pencil and ruler. We went for triangles and squares but choose whatever shapes you like. You'll find straight-sided shapes are easier to cut out. On a cutting mat, use the scalpel and a steel ruler to cut out the shapes. Then use the scalpel to divide the card up into individual stencils for each shape. Be sure to leave a good edge around each one. This will help when you come to the stencilling.

2 Use newspaper or scrap paper to line the inside of your cushion cover. Then place your first stencil on the cushion. Dab the paintbrush into the first ink colour and, holding the brush upright to the cushion, dab the brush over the stencil until it is covered. Gently remove the stencil to avoid any bleeding. Repeat this process with the same stencil a few more times in different places around the cushion.

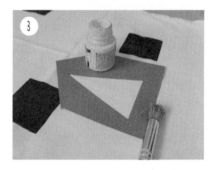

3 Now wash and dry your brush, wait for the first layer to dry completely, then pick another stencil and get ready to do your next layer of shapes.

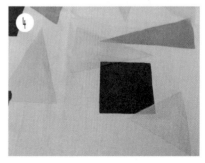

4 Repeat until all of your shapes and ink colours have been used.

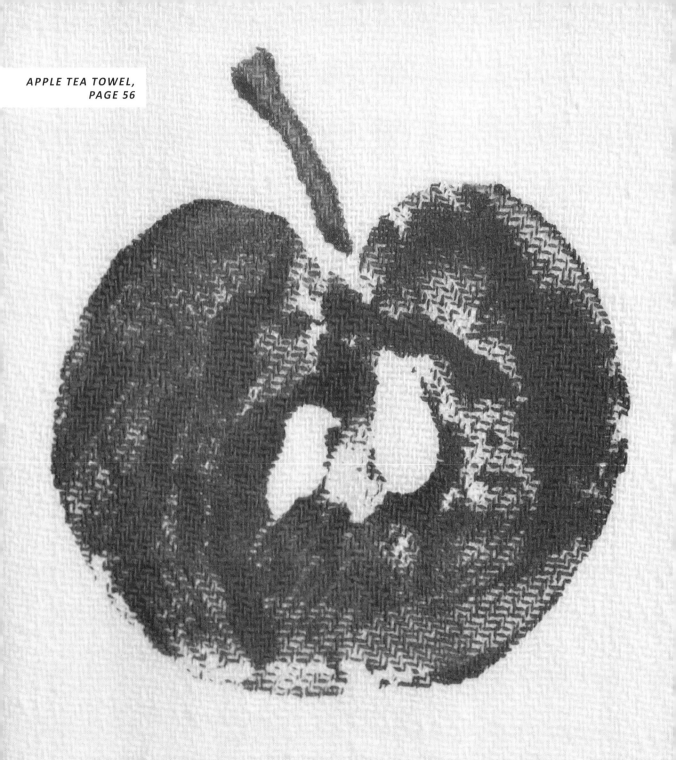

APPLE TEA TOWEL,
PAGE 56

GEOMETRIC CUSHION,
PAGE 42

RSVP invitations

WHAT YOU NEED

- ☐ Plain cards
- ☐ Embroidery hoop
- ☐ 43T mesh count silk
- ☐ Cutting mat
- ☐ Scalpel
- ☐ Screen-printing ink
- ☐ Old credit card
- ☐ Pencil
- ☐ Brown paper
- ☐ Old teaspoon

Remind your friends of your upcoming party with this smart update on the classic RSVP card. They'd be fools to miss it!

1   Start by tracing the RSVP design onto a piece of brown paper (template on page 114). Using the cutting mat and scalpel, slowly cut out the design. This design is quite intricate so take your time and always cut away from you, making sure to move the paper rather than twisting your arm too much.

2   Once the design has been cut out it's time to create your DIY screen. Start by opening out the hoop and laying a square of silk over the top. Then place the second part of the hoop over the silk and tighten the hoop until the silk has no lumps or bumps.

3   Now place your card onto a piece of newspaper or scrap paper to protect your work surface. Add the brown paper on top, positioning the design in the centre of the card. Centre the hoop screen on top, so that the silk is against the brown paper. Using an old teaspoon, blob a line of your chosen ink along the edge of the design. Then get an old credit card ready to use as a squeegee.

4   Pushing firmly, drag the credit card over the design, pulling the ink with it. As you pull over the design you will be able to see how even the coverage is. If you feel that it has not covered very well, pull the squeegee over the design again. Now slowly lift off the hoop and peel back the brown paper to reveal your hand-printed invitation. You can now repeat this process until you have printed enough cards for all your guests. Once you are finished, store your cards in a safe place to dry. They should be dry within an hour, but if they feel tacky to the touch then leave them a bit longer before you write on them.

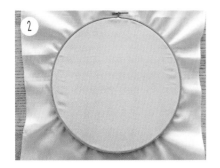

Tip! If you cut out more than one design from the brown paper and use different pieces of silk, you can print lots of different colours.

Daytripper backpack

X marks the spot with this striking hand-stamped project. The design is fun and slightly freestyle with only a few potatoes harmed along the way!

WHAT YOU NEED

- [ ] Canvas rucksack in a light colour
- [ ] Potato
- [ ] Sharp knife
- [ ] Pencil
- [ ] Sponge roller
- [ ] Fabric ink

Tip! This project would work well with lots of different shapes. If crosses aren't your thing, then try triangles, circles, squares or even arrows.

1 Cut the potato in half and draw the cross shape (see page 109) onto it using your pencil. Now carefully use the knife to start creating your printing block. Take your time. The best way to do this is to work in small sections. When cutting the block out make sure the cross section remains flat. This will ensure an even print.

2 Squeeze some fabric ink onto an old plate or palette, then take the sponge roller, roll it in the ink and then lightly roll onto your potato.

3 Once your potato is loaded with ink you can make your first print. Hold the ink side down on the top left of the bag and push down firmly. Now reveal your first cross. Repeat this process until the bag is evenly covered. Leave to dry before popping your essentials in and taking to the streets.

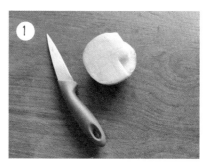

Segments t-shirt

This project gives you a quick and easy way to upcycle an old T-shirt and bring it back into your wardrobe rotation. Stamp printing works on all types of fabric, so you could jazz up a tired old skirt or an old sweater too.

WHAT YOU NEED

- ☐ Old T-shirt
- ☐ Fabric ink
- ☐ Scalpel or craft knife
- ☐ Pencil
- ☐ Potato
- ☐ Brown paper or newspaper

1 Cut the potato in half to leave a smooth surface. Then use your pencil to mark the half-circle shape on your potato.

2 Use your scalpel or craft knife to cut around the half-circle shape. Cut only to a depth of about ⅜in (1cm) into the potato, leaving you a handy little stamp.

3 You are now ready to print. Line the inside of your T-shirt with some brown paper or newspaper. Pour some fabric ink onto an old plate or palette and have your stamp to hand and ready to go.

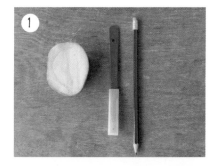

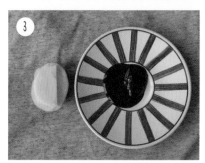

4   Dip your potato into the ink, stamp
    side down. Don't push it down
    too heavily; you only need a light
    coverage on the stamp.

5   Now press the potato stamp onto the
    bottom edge of the T-shirt, hold for
    a few seconds and release to reveal
    your stamp. You should have enough
    ink left on the stamp to move along
    and do the next print too.

6   After every second or third stamp, dip
    the potato back into the ink and work
    along the whole of the bottom edge
    of the T-shirt.

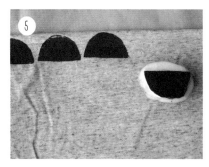

7   Repeat the process in a second line
    across the width of the T-shirt. We've
    printed five lines but you can do as
    many or as few as you like. Once dry,
    you need to fix the ink with a bit of
    heat by covering with a cloth and
    ironing over the design. The T-shirt
    can then be washed and worn over
    and over again.

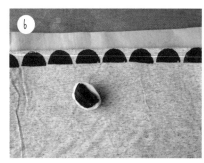

*Tip! Why not experiment
with other shapes or different
coloured fabric inks?*

RAINDROP BABY
SLEEPSUIT, PAGE 40

DINO TOTE BAG, PAGE 58

Apple tea towel

This project may remind you of school days but the effect is definitely bright and stylish, not childish!

WHAT YOU NEED

- [ ] Cotton tea towel
- [ ] Apple
- [ ] Knife
- [ ] Tweezers
- [ ] Red and green fabric ink

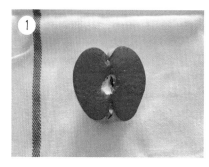

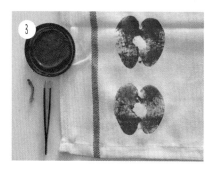

1 Start by covering your work surface with newspaper, then lay your tea towel down flat. Cut the apple in half and keep the stem to one side. Pour the red ink into an old saucer and dip the apple in it.

2 Push the apple firmly onto the bottom left corner of the tea towel. Hold for a few seconds. Repeat this step and print up the left-hand side of the tea towel.

3 Using tweezers, dip the apple stem into the green ink and print the stem onto each apple print. Once the ink is dry, seal it by covering with a cloth or paper and ironing.

Tip! You could try using pears to make a pair of fruity tea towels!

Dino tote bag

We all know day-to-day chores can be a bore, so add some fun to your shopping trip by jollying up a plain tote with this vibrant dinosaur screen print.

WHAT YOU NEED

- ☐ Cotton tote bag
- ☐ Piece of plain or tracing paper
- ☐ Adhesive tape
- ☐ Cutting mat
- ☐ Scalpel
- ☐ Pencil
- ☐ Brown paper
- ☐ Fabric ink
- ☐ 43T mesh count silk screen
- ☐ Squeegee

1 Start by tracing the dinosaur design (template on page 116) onto plain paper or tracing paper. Next, attach the paper to the centre of the brown paper using a bit of adhesive tape in each corner to secure it. Place the brown paper onto the cutting mat, grab your scalpel and start to cut out each section of the design. Once you have cut the design out, remove the top layer of paper. Your brown paper printing stencil has been made!

2 Position the stencil on the tote bag. We put our design on the bottom centre but you can place your design anywhere you like on your bag.

3 Now lay your screen over the design, making sure that the inside of the screen is covering only the brown paper and not the rest of the bag.

4 Blob some ink along the top of the design, then use a squeegee to pull the ink over the entire design. You can now reveal your freshly printed dino bag. Once it's dry, iron on the reverse to seal the ink in.

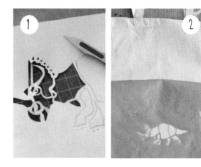

Tip! Ask a friend to hold the screen down firmly as you pull over the design to create a crisp print.

* < * > *

perpetual creative

* < * > *

Utensils apron

WHAT YOU NEED

- [ ] Plain cotton apron
- [ ] Craft knife or scalpel
- [ ] 2 sheets of brown paper about A3 size
- [ ] 2 sheets of tracing paper
- [ ] Pencil
- [ ] Adhesive tape
- [ ] Fabric ink in black and red
- [ ] Cutting mat
- [ ] Silk screen
- [ ] Squeegee
- [ ] Spoon

Inspired by a love for all things retro, this two-colour project will push your screen-printing skills to the next level. Play around with different colour combinations to change the look.

1 Trace the design onto a piece of tracing paper with a pencil (templates on pages 112–113). Label different sections of the template A or B, depending on whether they will be black or red. Stick it onto your first sheet of brown paper using a small piece of adhesive tape in each corner to secure it. Now, on the cutting mat, cut out all shapes marked 'A' with the craft knife.

2 Remove the tracing paper to reveal your brown paper stencil for the black areas. Where any pieces have become separate, use staples or tape to hold them in place.

3 Stick the tracing paper template onto the second sheet of brown paper and cut out all shapes marked 'B', as before. Take off the tracing paper to reveal your red ink stencil.

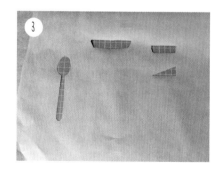

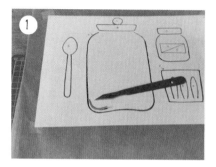

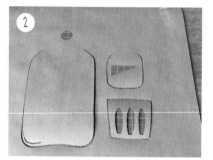

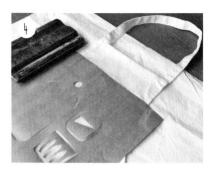

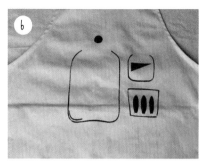

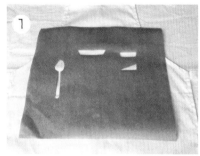

4 Lay your apron right side up on a protected flat surface and place the first stencil on top.

5 Put your screen on top, making sure all unmasked areas are visible so you can avoid inking the wrong spot. Spoon a line of black ink onto the screen at the top of your stencil covering the length of your design. Pull the squeegee towards you firmly and smoothly.

6 Remove the screen and check that the print is OK. Hang the apron to dry.

7 Remove the soggy brown paper stencil from the screen and discard it. Wash and dry your screen and make sure your first print is also dry. Line up the red ink stencil so that the pattern looks like the original image and place it on top of the apron as before.

8 Place the screen on top and repeat the printing process using red ink.

9 Remove the screen and brown paper stencil and dry the apron. Wash the screen. Once the apron is dry, iron your print on the wrong side to seal the design and make the apron machine washable.

Tip! Use some ink on a fine paintbrush to fill in any areas of the print that you might have missed.

ICONS PICNIC BLANKET, PAGE 68

UTENSILS APRON, PAGE 62

Icons picnic blanket

The perfect blanket for guys and gals on the go. Specifically designed to fit on the back of your bicycle, with this blanket you'll be prepared for spontaneous picnics wherever you go.

WHAT YOU NEED

- ☐ Heavy-duty blanket with a flat surface
- ☐ Silk screen
- ☐ Plain or tracing paper
- ☐ Brown paper slightly bigger than your screen
- ☐ Adhesive tape
- ☐ Cutting mat
- ☐ Craft knife or scalpel
- ☐ Pencil
- ☐ Scissors
- ☐ White fabric paint
- ☐ Squeegee

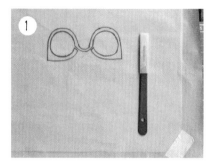

1 Trace your icons onto plain paper (templates on pages 110, 111 and 114). Stick the icons onto the sheet of brown paper using small pieces of tape at the corners. Arrange them as we have in picture 3, or however you like. The only limit is that they must fit within the area of the screen.

2 Use the craft knife or scalpel to cut out all the icon shapes. Take your time and turn the whole paper to help you navigate the curves neatly.

3 Once you have cut out all the pieces, trim the brown paper sheet to the size of the screen.

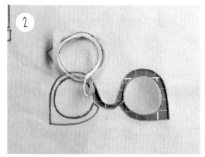

4 Place the template on top of the blanket in the top right-hand corner with the screen on top. Spoon ink along the top edge of your screen. In two downward strokes, pull the squeegee towards you to spread the ink evenly. Try not to overlap the strokes and use firm pressure. Lift the screen up, keeping the stencil intact.

5 Reposition the stencil and screen next to where you just printed. The number of times you will have to repeat the printing process depends on the size of your blanket. Cover the whole surface with evenly spaced repeats, working methodically in rows. Leave to dry overnight, then iron on the reverse to seal the ink.

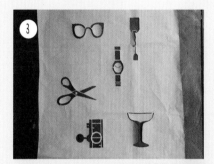

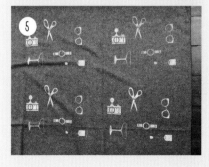

Tip! A little of this ink goes a long way so do not overload the screen.

Cuckoo clock art print

We have chosen a silhouette style to update this rather traditional cuckoo clock art print. Give it a personal touch by adding hand-painted details.

WHAT YOU NEED

- [ ] A4 piece of cotton calico fabric
- [ ] Tracing paper
- [ ] Brown paper
- [ ] Scalpel
- [ ] Cutting mat
- [ ] Fabric ink
- [ ] Cocktail stick
- [ ] Squeegee
- [ ] Silk screen
- [ ] Adhesive tape
- [ ] Pencil with an eraser

1   Start by tracing the clock design onto a piece of A4 size tracing paper (template on page 108). Stick the four corners of the tracing paper onto your brown paper using small pieces of adhesive tape. Use the scalpel to cut out the centre circle of the clock and the window details and hang on to them. Then cut out the rest of the design.

2   Lay your calico on some newspaper and place your brown paper stencil on top. Now take your clock circle and window details and place them inside the stencil in the correct places as shown.

3   Now carefully lay your screen over the design, making sure the loose parts stay in the right place. Use a spoon to spread the black fabric ink at the top of the design.

Tip! Choose another colour of ink for the chains to add contrast, or stick with the same colour for a monochrome look.

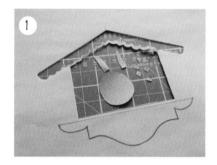

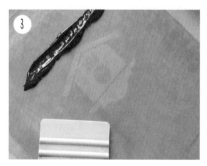

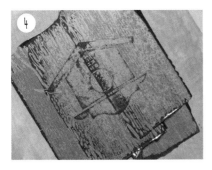

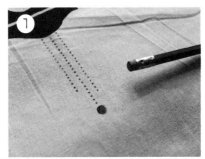

4   Ask someone to hold your screen down for you as you use the squeegee to pull the ink over the design until it is fully covered.

5   Lift the screen and peel off the stencil to reveal your print. Leave to dry.

6   Once dry, dab your cocktail stick into the green ink and use a piece of scrap paper as a guide for your chains. Gently dab little dots in a long line to create your first chain.

7   Repeat this two more times, varying the length of each chain. Dab the eraser on your pencil into the ink and use to print a circle in the middle of the clock face and at the end of the centre chain. Using your cocktail stick again, choose your time and mark it out. We chose 4pm, the perfect time for a tea break!

Chevron place mats

Stencil-printed cork mats make a retro classic into a graphic must-have. For an extra twist use a metallic paint as a contrast. Perfect for jazzing up your table.

WHAT YOU NEED

- ☐ Cork place mats
- ☐ Masking tape
- ☐ Pencil
- ☐ Stencil brush
- ☐ Scissors
- ☐ Acrylic paint
- ☐ Tape measure
- ☐ Plate or palette

1 Start by cutting your masking tape into 17 strips of 2 ¾in (7cm) long.

2 Now use the tape measure to find the centre of your cork place mat. Mark the place with a small pencil dot.

3 Stick your first piece of masking tape to the cork mat, using the dot you made as a marker for the top left-hand corner of the masking tape. Using your tape measure, mark a vertical line down the masking tape as shown.

4 Now stick the next piece of masking tape over the top of the first, creating an upside down V shape. The line you have just drawn acts as a guideline to ensure it is being stuck down evenly.

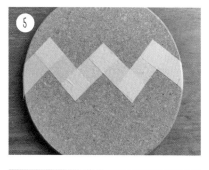

5 Repeat this process across the middle of the mat to create a zigzag effect.

6 Leaving a gap that is the same distance as the width of the tape, start your next line of masking tape zigzags in the same way.

7 Now do the same at the top of the mat, leaving you with an even coverage of zigzags.

8 You are now ready to paint. Blob out a little paint onto an old plate or palette.

9 Take your stencil brush and dab it into the paint. Holding the brush vertically to the mat, dab the paint onto the exposed cork areas.

10 Keep going across the whole middle section. Then do the same for the bottom and top, taking care to paint an even coverage.

11 You may find you need to add an extra coat depending on how water-based your paint is, so leave it to dry and assess the situation after an hour or so. Once you are happy with how it looks and the paint is dry, slowly peel off the masking tape.

12 Repeat this process on the rest of your cork mats until you have as many as you need.

Brogue-effect canvas shoes

Add interest to a plain pair of shoes with our mixed technique 'brogue-ing' project. This perfect alternative to a smart summer shoe will add a bright pop of colour to any outfit.

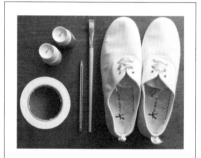

WHAT YOU NEED

- [ ] Pair of white canvas shoes
- [ ] Paintbrush
- [ ] New pencil with eraser
- [ ] Masking tape
- [ ] Fabric painting ink in blue and white

Tip! Using a paintbrush with a square end makes adding the diagonal lines a lot easier.

1 Start by lightly drawing your brogue design onto the shoes using a pencil. Use the photographs as a guide.

2 Stick some masking tape along the sides to protect the sole and create a neat, even line. Dip your paintbrush into the blue fabric ink and start to gently paint in the blocked areas.

3 Paint in all the blocked areas and leave to dry.

4 Once dry, it's time to print your brogue detailing. Start with the wing tips and, using the eraser on the end of your pencil, gently dip the eraser into the white ink and hold for a few seconds on the shoes. The key here is not to push too hard otherwise the ink will spread. Finally add a row of blue spots across under the laces. Leave to dry, then step out in style in your brand-new, customized shoes.

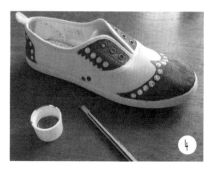

committed crafter

Greetings banner

WHAT YOU NEED

- [ ] Old tote bag
- [ ] Scalpel or craft knife
- [ ] Adhesive tape
- [ ] Piece of A4 card
- [ ] Piece of A4 paper
- [ ] Cutting mat
- [ ] Stencil brush
- [ ] Pinking shears
- [ ] Fabric scissors
- [ ] Fabric ink in three colours
- [ ] Dowelling
- [ ] String

Mixing inks to create a cool ombré, or graduated colour, effect in this stencil print is a fun way to create a feature wall while playing around with a message of your own. Perfect for a thrifty crafter who loves an upcycling project.

1 Draw your design onto plain paper or type it and print it out in a large size so it fills the page. Tape the design onto the piece of card. The best way to do this is to add a little piece of adhesive tape in each corner.

2 Using your cutting mat to work on, cut out the stencil with your scalpel or craft knife.

3 Use the fabric scissors to carefully remove the handles of your tote bag and discard.

4   Now, using the fabric scissors, cut up the sides of the tote bag and along the bottom so that you end up with two rectangular pieces of fabric with hems along the top edge. You will need only one piece for this project.

5   Lay one of the rectangles onto a protected work surface and place the card stencil onto the centre of it. Secure with adhesive tape on all four sides of the stencil.

6   Pour out three blobs of your chosen inks onto an old plate or palette and make sure your stencil brush is clean.

7   Using your first colour, begin to stipple over the top of the stencil. Make sure the paint coverage becomes lighter as you move down the banner. Wash and dry your brush, then use your second colour to mix into the first colour to start to create the ombré effect. It's best to start with the darkest colour and then use a lighter colour. We used white as the second colour.

8   Wash and dry your brush again and use your third ink, starting from the bottom of the stencil this time. Use a dabbing technique to control the ombré effect.

9   Wash your brush again, then work the second and third ink colours up into the middle section of the stencil. Use the second colour primarily but ensure there is a hint of the other two colours for an effective ombré look.

10 Carefully remove your stencil from the fabric to reveal your print and set it aside to dry.

11 Now use your pinking shears to cut the corners off the bottom of the banner so that it forms a V shape.

12 Poke your dowelling through the hem that was at the top of the bag.

13 Cut a piece of string about as long as your arm (or long if you like) and tie it onto both ends of the dowelling. Your banner is now ready to hang.

Tip! After applying the first colour, you can speed up the drying process by using a hairdryer.

GREETINGS BANNER, PAGE 82

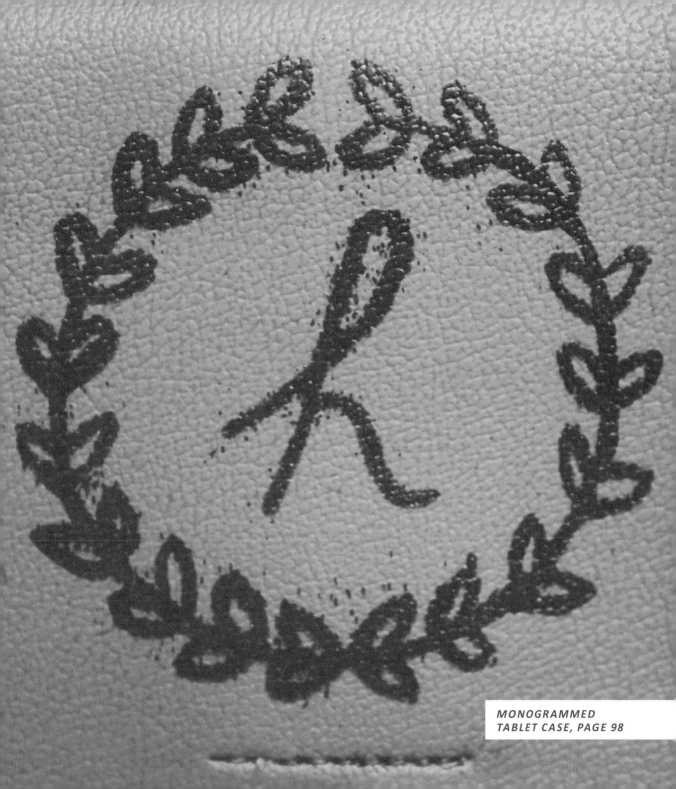

MONOGRAMMED
TABLET CASE, PAGE 98

Retro lampshade

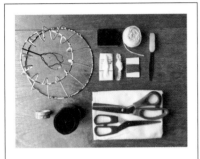

This is one for the textile lovers and is a slightly more technical project. Try to source some second-hand or vintage fabric to give this 1950s-inspired print a little extra authenticity.

WHAT YOU NEED

- [ ] Old birdcage-style lampshade frame
- [ ] Up to 39in (1m) of plain white fabric
- [ ] Scissors
- [ ] Pinking shears
- [ ] Pins
- [ ] Fabric ink or paint
- [ ] Sponge roller
- [ ] Small wooden block
- [ ] Cotton string
- [ ] Embroidery needle and sharp
- [ ] Thread
- [ ] 39in (1m) ribbon
- [ ] Tape measure

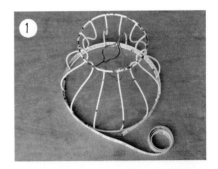

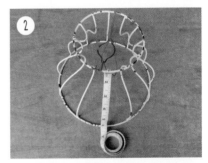

1 Remove any remains of old fabric covering your lampshade frame. Measure the top and bottom diameters of the lampshade. The biggest measurement will be the length to cut the fabric to.

2 Now measure the height of the lampshade. Once you have these two measurements, you need to add ⅝in (1.5cm) at each end for the seam allowance.

3 To make the stamp take a 20in (0.5m) long piece of string and wrap it around the width of your wooden block and tie in a double knot at the back. Then wind the string around the block about eight times. Move the string around a little until you are happy with the spacing.

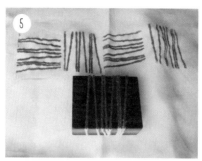

4   Pour some ink onto an old plate and load up your sponge roller.

5   Working from left to right or vice versa, print in straight lines across the length of your fabric. Turn the block 90° to the left and right between each print to alternate between horizontal stripes and vertical stripes.

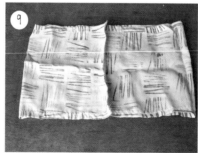

6   Once you have covered the entire surface, hang the fabric up to dry. You can speed up the drying process with a hairdryer.

7   Pin ⅝in (1.5cm) hems along the longest sides of the fabric, which will be the top and bottom of your lampshade. Later these will be used to thread a drawstring through to fit the fabric to the frame.

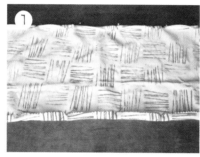

8   Sew along the length using straight stitches in a colour of thread that matches the fabric. You could use a machine for this if you have one. Secure at each end by sewing a few stitches backward and forward at the start and finish.

9   Now, with the right sides together, pin the two short ends together and sew ⅝in (1.5cm) in from top to bottom. Secure in the same way as you did in step 8.

Tip! Sponge rollers are cheap and are the best way to spread your ink evenly, especially on bumpy surfaces such as this string creation.

10 Now press the fabric to fix the ink and remove any creases, then turn your tube the right side facing out. Check it fits over the largest part of the frame, then remove again. Using your embroidery needle, thread long lengths of string through the top and bottom hems, gathering as you go.

11 Place the fabric over the frame and pull the strings to gather around the top and the bottom edges of the frame, securing with a bow.

12 Take your ribbon and tie it around the neck of the shade to pull the fabric into shape. Finally, readjust the string at each opening before knotting securely and trimming any excess length off.

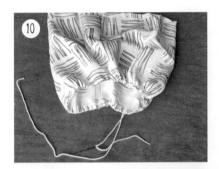

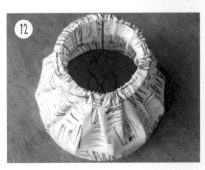

Monochrome jute rug

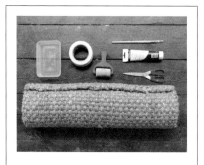

WHAT YOU NEED

- ☐ Woven rug, preferably made from a natural fibre
- ☐ Masking tape
- ☐ Scissors
- ☐ Black acrylic paint
- ☐ Small sponge roller
- ☐ Flat medium-sized paintbrush
- ☐ Plastic container for mixing

If you are looking for a bold way to welcome visitors into your home, our statement printed rug might be just what you need. Simple, striking and oh-so versatile.

1 Use three small pieces of masking tape to mark the centre and quarter points of your rug.

2 Now run three long lengths of tape all the way from top to bottom, dividing the surface into four sections.

3 Using shorter lengths of tape, mask in the chevron design from top to bottom.

4 Continue masking in the chevron design from right to left.

5 Mask the last section in diagonal diamond shapes.

6 Now squeeze about half your tube of acrylic paint into the container. Try to keep it at one end so you have space to load up the roller smoothly.

7 Starting from the top right corner and working on a small area at a time, roll the paint onto the rug. You will need to use quite a heavy pressure to give an even coverage.

8 Once you have covered the entire surface, leave the paint to dry for at least one hour. If you are not happy with any of the coverage, use your paintbrush to fill in any extra gaps.

9 After an hour, remove the tape carefully and leave to dry overnight.

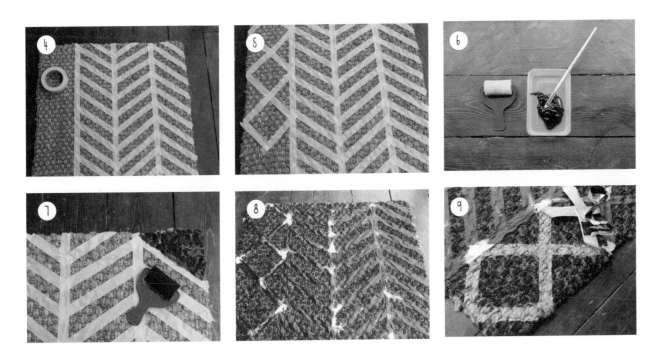

Tip! Use the flat paintbrush to help even out the paint coverage on the roller if it seems a bit heavier on one side. This will help give a more even coverage when applying paint.

MULTI-PRINT WALLPAPER,
PAGE 102

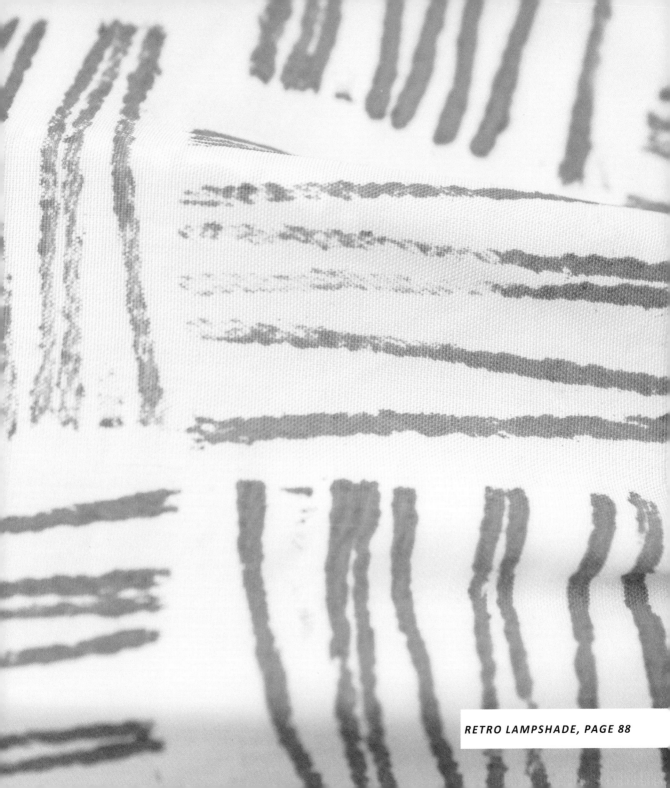

RETRO LAMPSHADE, PAGE 88

Monogrammed tablet case

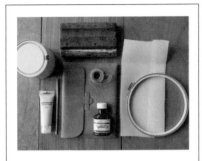

WHAT YOU NEED

- [ ] Plain tablet case
- [ ] Embroidery hoop
- [ ] 43T mesh count silk
- [ ] Drawing fluid
- [ ] Small paintbrush
- [ ] Adhesive tape
- [ ] Screen block
- [ ] Squeegee
- [ ] Fabric paint or acrylic paint (depending on your tablet case material)

A contemporary way to identify your technology indeed! In this project we have tried to rework a traditional idea without losing the character of the original style. The DIY screen means you can monogram your favourite items over and over again.

1 First design your monogram using ours as a guide (template on page 109) and copy it onto a piece of thin paper with marker pen. You want the design to show through the paper. Next make your screen by opening up your embroidery hoop and laying the silk inside. Do the hoop up as tight as you can, pulling the silk as tight around the hoop. Tape the stencil face up on the underside of the screen.

2 Turn the hoop over and trace the backwards design on the top of the silk with a pencil.

3 Dip your paintbrush in the drawing fluid and start to paint your design on the top of the silk. You don't need much ink at all as a little goes a long way. Take your time and do this neatly. Leave to dry overnight.

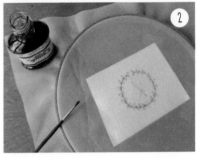

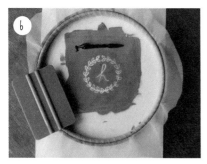

4 Once dry, spoon out some screen block and lay it along the top of your design on the top of the screen.

5 Use your squeegee to spread the block over the entire design. Leave to dry overnight.

6 The next day, use warm water to wash the screen. The aim here is to reveal your design, so wash with care and use a small sponge to reveal some areas if they are being too stubborn. Leave the screen to dry or give it a good blast with a hairdryer. Once your 'exposed screen' is ready, turn the hoop the other way round and spoon some ink along the top of the design.

7 Now place the screen onto your tablet case and pull the squeegee over the design. Remove the screen carefully to reveal your monogram and leave to dry.

Tip! Once you have made your screen you can add your monogram to almost anything you fancy.

Multi-print wallpaper

Use traditional lino-print skills to create a feature wall to
be proud of. Our paper-chain wallpaper is ideal for the office,
a children's playroom or your bedroom.

WHAT YOU NEED

- [ ] Paper to copy designs on to
- [ ] Plain white wallpaper
- [ ] Scissors
- [ ] Lino roller
- [ ] Two types of lino sheets – traditional thick lino and backed easy-cut lino
- [ ] Craft knife
- [ ] Lino-cutting tool
- [ ] Painting sponge
- [ ] Small paintbrush
- [ ] Small wooden block
- [ ] Superglue
- [ ] Masking tape
- [ ] Pencil
- [ ] Acrylic paints in two colours

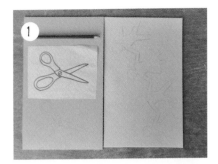

1 Use a pencil to trace the scissors and people patterns onto paper (templates on pages 114–115). Transfer the scissors stencil onto thick lino and the people stencil onto easy-cut lino by drawing heavily over the template so that you make an indent on the lino.

2 Use the craft knife to score around the outline of the scissors motif.

3 With the lino-cutting tool, scrape away inside the scissors' handles. Then use the craft knife to carefully define the rest of the scissors detail.

4 Use the lino-cutting tool to scrape away around the outside of the motif. Scoring with the knife first means you should get a nice clean line.

Tip! Be careful when using the lino tool that you don't slip and scrape away the wrong bit. Slow and steady wins the race!

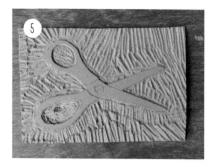

5 Scrape away all the rest of the lino surface and trim down the excess if required.

6 For the paper people, you can cut the entire piece out of the easy-cut lino using very sharp scissors.

7 Cut three random triangles from the easy-cut lino and glue haphazardly onto your wooden block.

8 Now all three motifs are complete, lay a length of wallpaper onto a table or flat surface and stick it down at the corners using adhesive tape.

9 Start with the scissors motif. This works best if you dilute the acrylic paint with a bit of water. Apply slightly diluted paint to the raised motif using the painting sponge.

10 Press the motif into place paint side down and apply medium pressure with the roller.

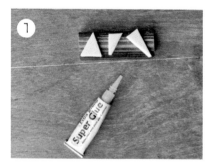

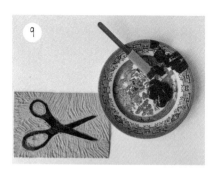

Tip! Use your fingertips to push down onto the template if you find the roller is moving it around.

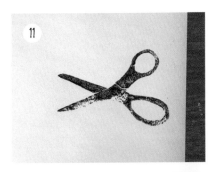

11 Lift the lino up, being careful not to smudge the paint.

12 Repeat this process along the length of your paper, alternating from one side to another, spacing them evenly.

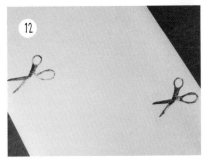

13 Next, using undiluted acrylic paint, spread an even coat onto the lino people print and place the piece carefully, face down, next to the scissors design. With an even pressure, run the rubber roller over the people print. Now repeat this next to the other scissors prints all along the length of your wallpaper.

14 Now take a bright colour of acrylic paint and apply it using your brush to the triangles on your block stamp.

15 Beneath each pair of scissors, stamp the triangles three times in different directions to achieve a haphazard scattered affect. Repeat the process on as many sheets of wallpaper as you need.

······ **bits and bobs** ······

Templates

Cuckoo clock art print, page 70
Copy this at 200%

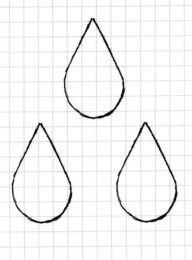

Raindrop baby sleepsuit, page 40
Copy this at 100%

Monogrammed tablet case, page 98
Copy this at 100%

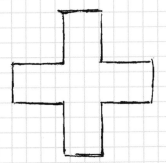

Daytripper backpack, page 48
Copy this at 100%

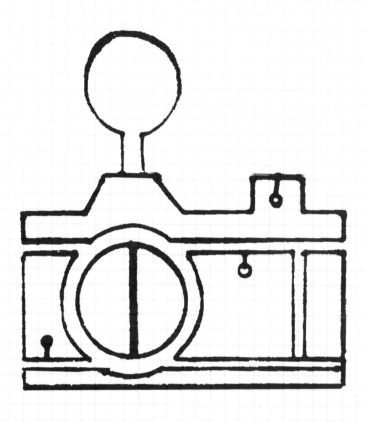

Icons picnic blanket, page 68   Copy this at 100%

Icons picnic blanket, page 68   Copy these at 100%

Utensils apron, page 62
Copy this at 150%

Utensils apron, page 62
Copy these at 150%

RSVP invitations, page 46   Copy this at 100%

RSVP

Icons picnic blanket, page 68
Copy this at 100%

Multi-print wallpaper, page 102
Copy this at 150%

Multi-print wallpaper, page 102
Copy this at 150%

Dino tote bag, page 58
Copy this at 100%

Resources

supplies

ArtiFolk
www.artifolk.co.uk

Clarkes Office Supplies
www.clarkesofficesupplies.co.uk

eBay
www.ebay.co.uk

Etsy
www.etsy.com

Farrow and Ball
www.farrow-ball.com

Hobbycraft
www.hobbycraft.co.uk

Kemptown Flea Market and Lewes Flea Market
www.flea-markets.co.uk

Not on the High Street
www.notonthehighstreet.com

Spinsters Emporium
www.spinstersemporium.co.uk

WHSmith
www.whsmith.co.uk

inspiration

Brighton Artists
www.aoh.org.uk

Craftgawker
craftgawker.com

Craftivism and the Craftivist Collective
craftivist-collective.com

The Crafts Council
www.craftscouncil.org.uk

Ditchling Museum of Art & Craft
www.ditchlingmuseumartcraft.org.uk

Kinfolk
www.kinfolk.com

Oh Comely
www.ohcomely.co.uk

Selvedge
www.selvedge.org

Stylegawker
stylegawker.com

events

Made Brighton craft fair
www.brighton-made.co.uk

Top Drawer London
www.topdrawer.co.uk

Acknowledgements

This book has come about after several years of hard slog, of faces new and old imparting information, advice and support, whether it be big or small – a phone call or a even just a hello. To the many friends, family members and loved ones who have come and gone through the whirlwind that is setting up your own business as women in industry, we want to say thank you.

Knowing us there is probably a lot more we have said over these short years and sometimes we have been known to say too much, but without you we would not have stuck at it, this our dream project.

It would be unfair to name a few special people as there are so many that have been involved and inspired us, so we'd like to say thank you for friendship. Because that inevitably is what it always comes back to.

We'd also like to thank everyone at GMC for believing in our brand.

Index

To order a book, or to request a catalogue, contact: GMC Publications Ltd,
Castle Place, 166 High Street, Lewes, East Sussex, BN7 1XU, United Kingdom
Tel: +44 (0)1273 488005

www.gmcbooks.com